Graphite

The BreakBeat Poets series

ABOUT THE BREAKBEAT POETS SERIES

The BreakBeat Poets series, curated by Kevin Coval and Nate Marshall, is committed to work that brings the aesthetic of hip-hop practice to the page. These books are a cipher for the fresh, with an eye always to the next. We strive to center and showcase some of the most exciting voices in literature, art, and culture.

BREAKBEAT POETS SERIES TITLES INCLUDE:

The BreakBeat Poets: New American Poetry in the Age of Hip-Hop, edited by Kevin Coval, Quraysh Ali Lansana, and Nate Marshall

This Is Modern Art: A Play, Idris Goodwin and Kevin Coval

The Breakbeat Poets Vol. 2: Black Girl Magic, edited by Mahogany L. Browne, Jamila Woods, and Idrissa Simmonds

Human Highlight, Idris Goodwin and Kevin Coval

On My Way to Liberation, H. Melt

Black Queer Hoe, Britteney Black Rose Kapri

Citizen Illegal, José Olivarez

The BreakBeat Poets Vol. 3: Halal if You Hear Me, edited by Fatimah Asghar and Safia Elhillo

There Are Trans People Here, H. Melt

Commando, E'mon Lauren

Graphite

Patricia Frazier

Haymarket Books
Chicago, IL

Published in 2018 by
Haymarket Books
P.O. Box 180165
Chicago, IL 60618
www.haymarketbooks.org

ISBN: 978-1-64259-000-5

Trade distribution:
In the US, Consortium Book Sales and Distribution, www.cbsd.com
In Canada, Publishers Group Canada, www.pgcbooks.ca
In the UK, Turnaround Publisher Services, www.turnaround-uk.com
All other countries, Ingram Publisher Services International,
IPS_Intlsales@ingramcontent.com

This book was published with the generous support of Lannan Foundation and
Wallace Action Fund.

Cover artwork by Fantasia A. Graham.
Cover design by Eric Kerl.

Printed in Canada by union labor.

Library of Congress Cataloging-in-Publication data is available.

10 9 8 7 6 5 4 3 2 1

They win sometimes, they lose sometimes, they've been injured, they've been happy, they've been sad, ignored, booed mightily . . . , they've been cheered, and through it all and evident to all were those people who are enraged they are there at all—graphite against a sharp white background.

—Claudia Rankine

To my grandmothers.
Dede, you were Graphite, my favorite Black girl.
Granny Lucy, I'm sorry for everything you'll find out in this book.

Contents

Graphite Made It!

rolled right out
of the packaging
and kissed her country's
toes.

Graphite never read
Langston Hughes,
but knows: *One should love*
one's country, for one's country is
your mama.

Graphite's mama
does not love her back,
That's against
God Pat Pat rolls back up
Graphite's throat.

Graphite has five kids,
two of them died,
became gravel
underneath her tongue,

Graphite forgets
to take her insulin.
Graphite has blood thick
with everything
she can't remember.

Graphite drinks the good brew
and a soldier spills from her chest.
She lets the old body drop
quicksand through the bathroom
floor.

Graphite dies.
goes back to the projects.
She never wanted to leave.
Graphite loves her country.

Graphite knows her job,
to be Black,
and erasable.
Graphite does it well.

Auditioning for the Role
of Child with Teen Parent

look, I know a Vice special when I see one. it looks like me and my
    Mama,
curled up on the twin in the back of Graphite's apartment: sixteen and
    prayer,
queens of the WIC wasteland.

MTV thinks equality means casting girls that don't look like me and
    my Mama.
I think we could use the check. we know what we're here for. working
    twice as hard
for a closed caption. we lighter fluid to a childhood, after-school special
    or recurring curse.

Still, I slay every role—the twice more likely. lucky accident. Gilmore
    Girl.
lady with the body that makes a mouth *PUT IT ON ERRTHANG,*
    SHE PREGNANT?
when I get arrogant, I remind myself I am only what can hide
inside of an oversized polo hoodie. I am seen but not here.
rich nigga, poor nigga, still a harrowing tale.

y'all late, I thought my Mama was badass before Kylie Jenner did it.
I never believed the hype of nine to five girls who had their head in the
    books
because every chapter was my Mama's name. I understand I'm audi-
    tioning
for a character, not writing the script, but I know this could be so
    much more.

I think my Mama is more beautiful than an anti-abortion billboard.

I think my conception is more radical than a stupid mistake.
what if she's a teenage mom and this is still a story about Black
    excellence?
she doesn't have to get her master's degree. she doesn't need a world
    class viola tour.
give my Mama a Pulitzer for losing the baby phat before prom. give my
    Mama a Pushcart
for the way she wrote my absence letter when I needed a day off. hear
    me out.

I know time is money, I know I'll get the part. I just want to pitch
    something first:
this could be a story about a Black girl from the projects, who has sex
    at sixteen
and gets pregnant, or it could just be a special about me and my Mama
eating Flamin' Hots on the couch at 12am. we understand what it
    could've been
but we're here now and we like it just fine.

Theme Song About Blk Love
in the Time of My Grandparents

for WLBJ

"We are a conspiracy." —Assata Shakur

all I want for my birthday is a sitcom
about Black love in the time of my Grandparents.
a thirty-minute pilot for Grandad's gold tooth
and red tux, posted up on 59th to spit game
at my Grandma.

I want the theme song dedicated to my Grandad's
eyes when he first saw her, stilettos
splintering sidewalk, a baby the '70s couldn't take.
I want the title of the show to be my Grandad's answer
to his mother-in-law's inquiry on what's wrong with Graphite:
She Just Needs a Little Love.

I want people to need to know the true story
of my grandparents,
the reason I know girls with
lithium prescriptions deserve love too.

my Granddad deserves a book of essays,
hardcover motown, extended edition.
his van a jukebox of Black history.
every Deniece Williams song
another detail about my Grandma.
the car stripped of her subtle hum
only reminds us of her absence.
he mourns his woman in collected vinyl crates.

My Grandpa calls my lover Old Man
and tells me I look especially like her today.
I wear sweatpants and drink a bottle of Fireball.
I lose a baby in the swig of a birth control pill
and wonder what if my grandparents were millennials?
would my Grandma have ever had Latoria,
a streetlight knocked out
in the wind of a snowstorm?
could my Granddad have found time
to cry for his child lost to incubator cold?
I wait for irony to stop claiming the people
I should get to know. I make love
and don't think
twice about a condom. I am sad
and hoping God will send me a little girl
for my Grandma,
I am hoping God will
chapbook my body into an after poem.
My lover holds me in the fold of his sweatshirt,
It is no red tux, but it gives me hope.

I am listening to an album of my grandparents,
love songs that bump black but not brutal.
my grandparents are conscious rap
my Grandpa didn't need high school experience
to know what healthy love looked like
my Grandma freedom fights with an eskimo kiss
a civil rights biopic in the kitchen
of my childhood.
all this revolution in making a house
full of more mouths to feed. no fear to bear sons.
loving despite the cops or psych ward,
my Grandparents rode the frontlines
of Black love and won.

Dorothy Goes Low-End Crazy

there's no place like it.
                              a boiled thermometer, bussin'.
      boys seep bloody from sidewalk cracks,
                              crabs in a bucket, heated seafood by
sunset.
                    '09 Chevy Impalas work emerald city,
          Boosie bumps from every speaker.
                              niggas in Pelles with tucked chains
                              meet at Mandrake Park
                              trap and talk shit on the court.
                                        I pop out the whip,
flossing,
hair blowing in the wind
              shake up by the tennis court
      and stalk the yellow brick.
knowing we are only little
hood girls pretending to be lions,

knowing our hearts beat too

                    bulging for these tin box bodies

we pray for Oakwood in pennies
      quiet drops of sweat thrown down a neck.
                              we hope Mandrake can ease
us down
                    a childhood without holes.
              we watch for signs of danger
          in the Totos on the court
                              we forget how to play.
all that's left is ground.

I remember the day we landed here
saucy in a pink Easter dress
kindergarten diplomas
rolled up
dress socks.
it was a celebration,
a communion of cousins.
what we didn't know
was this was the last
generation to stay
at school before it closed.

before the fefe we heard the fire blast,
the brick house bullet coming to claim
the witch of us with ruby Jays,
& sunset on our faces
we drowned
into plush play mats.

I closed my eyes and
clicked my heels
three times:
There's no place like the block.
There's no place like the block.
There's no place like the block.

Cousin Clarence Says Amen

his phantom feet singing across lake shore drive
granny tells the story like a Black Flash
her nephew swept away 60 mph
maybe someone's lucky accident
or reason for trauma
all the Wells Boys weeping tears
turned into tea for sipping
at everyone's kitchenette table
someone's mama tells his story
with the rough grab of an elbow

niggas shout when I jaywalk
or walk in big groups
or stop them from running a light
niggas just need reason to hit a Black kid
guilty adrenaline thirsty for all our juicy
blood against the white hood
of a dented Camaro
face frozen atop the ice cream paint job
left unscathed
we the reason for everything
the voodoo of our fuck up touch
deserves a witch trial, a hunt, a hanging
from the tonsils of our grandparents
for all the things wrong with our generation
                                        and the one before
and the one where Clarence didn't run
they never leave the crib
they sit until plastic covers bustle at their seams
they plan the beach trip until peach fuzz bubbles over
a twenty-one-year-old mouth:

the wish that keeps a childhood still.
the moment before the car hits
and you hear your Grandmother's china smash
all reasons Black kids should just stay home.

Twinkie Sold Tacos

out of her apartment,
specialized in thinning
pork in black cast iron.
handled the heat of metal
like no HotBoy could.
shredded the government
cheese into her greasy palm.
rolled sevens in the skillet.
that shit hit every time.

her cousin sold too.
product for the Hotboyz.
police raided the apartment
and Twinkie conjured
a kitchenette language
the pigs couldn't speak
thinned under the thunder
of her tongue.
Twinkie was a bad bitch.
Ida B. Wells renowned.

when cousin Toke died
the police raided his body
and blamed it on the Hotboyz.
The Wells made Twinkie
another weeping relative.
the city dropped a bomb on our
Black Wall Street.

the matriarch was evicted
and the whole building followed.

Applehead shut down
his candy store.
Keisha ain't takin hair appointments
in her apartment no more,
and it hits me.

My Uncle Was Born

Mercy
hospital became federal
prison
true story:
his umbilical cord cuffed his neck
a crystal ball choke
some folk only know
solitary confinement
nine months
he would carry
a penitentiary with him
wherever he went.

My Uncle teaches me how to trap.
finesse coin from Columbia kids
who don't know an eighth from an ounce.
My Uncle is cold metal
Chicago heavy
Emmett tongue, trouble boy.
his parole officer is facebook.
everything our family finds wrong
with the way he won't
let things go.
his body a casket
of tattoos,
039 crazy
RIP Auntie Julie
as long as my Uncle walks
The Wells will never be dead.
I think that makes him a freedom fighter.
I think his mother would be proud.

God Is a Cosmetologist

my GOD a cosmetologist. a scalp carpenter. salon technician for
Black boys dyed the wrong shade of red. always stitching things back
in place, THEY know the politic of braiding together a boxed-in
body of people, gerrymandered by a crooked part.

my GOD is brown JAM. holding the hood together when police
decide to bantu knot Black women, steal their right to remain loud
and laughing, drooling Hennessy puddles into the ground. homage
to dead homies whose cornrows weren't sewn tight enough to stop
their bodies from being split ends. when Tyrone's silk strands diddy
bopped in the basement party of a cemetery, all of the women in his
family wore weaves to the funeral.

my GOD a master of disguise. THEY were the first to find out why
camouflage invisible men. THEY know a beauty standard could be a
halo braid. THEY know self-love also exist in a bottle
of Maxi's Hair Glue, as it slimes onto the lashes of the street. spills
from the shed virgin Brazilian that tumbleweeds down the block
after another one of ours is twisted in.

my GOD cradles the buildings in a greasy hairnet, THEY know
that ghetto girls were carefree first, laying down the track, throwing
on the wig. doing your homegirl's feed-in for the low, because that's
love, the most protective style. preservation in the face of kink-wired
fence. a beauty supply as brass knuckles, a lace front to rip when the
bulldozers come.

A Poem for Englewood

Engle[1]	Wood[2]
Engle	wood/
Verb	*Noun*
1. To cajole or coax	1. an area of land covered with growing trees.

land of finesse. land of growing. giving birth. burning bush. Black belt. in redlining. urban planned and dictionary decoded noun: most ghetto neighborhood in all of Chicago

Englewood the bloody name nobody wants to have, but everybody wants to hold.

Englewood Teaches a Lesson in Pronunciation

I heard folks mistook it for Black death
made sacrilege of my name before stepping foot on my asphalt
I heard white kids been beatboxing my name in their poems
an imperialist jukebox produced by Fox News
they made a SoundCloud chopped and screwed
diss track of my body for street cred

a white girl called me a war zone but ate my name
in the trenches of her teeth   *anglewood*
my curves too obtuse to fit
comfortably between her lips

my name is something earned
a plus sized pilgrimage only bucket boys know
a covenant of closed schools and colored girls clawing their way out
my name is pleading no while Rahm does
what Daley did to my sister Hyde Park another
gentrified Black girl gone
but us Black girls don't be getting no amber alerts

bombed the first Black family
to make a home in my skin
gave up when there became more Black
people than bombs to throw
realized how to color-bomb through the tv screen
call it modern warfare technology
why you think anti-englewood rhetoric percolates
through Chicago bodies
a blood clot of BlackonBlack crime
while northside neighborhoods get to call their violence inter-communal

the whip of white savior wordplay
the Whole Foods is a grave plot
for those who couldn't be whited out
my name the tree that is soiling

the rest of the forest

cut down   hill   to a landfill

where white privilege plays Rahm the Builder
with my limbs
and nobody asks me for consent
before taking my name to make Chicago
the martyr they need her to be

I pray y'all make my name a good poem
a liquor store lacquer, a flash mob crip walk on Garfield
I pray somebody writes an ode to Englewood
turn my name into a city of God
a Black hole of Black girl resurrection

I raised a girl that wrote poems
heard she say my name real well
call me a non-perishable
if you've ever known me as anything else
you shouldn't be writing poems about Englewood

Graphite Receives Her Eviction

for Graphite so loved the world
she gave her only brain.
pearled tobacco in the paper of a ComEd bill
and lit it stovetop.
slumped naked in her pleather rocking chair
sweat and sticky-ass turned affirmation,
A bitch ain't got shit to give to nobody.
I can't even get a Black & Mild outta muthafuckas.
she shouted a sailor song at ABC 7,
a list of all the ways the first Black bachelorette
has fucked up so far. & this was the first day.

the second day she filed her fingernail into a Divacup
she'd decide what to make of her own blood.
she knew there was no heaven for women with
potty mouths.
if God was iffy about letting her in
she'd ready her own Red Sea.

the third day she built a beauty parlor
in her bathroom
inking a new set of jet black eyebrows
dotting a beauty mark in the top right corner
of her upper lip.
she could be Marilyn Monroe,
skirt up for no muthafucka
who didn't deserve a peek

until the fourth day.
we found her face down in the carpet.
no pants or recollection of a house.

begging someone to take her home.
maybe to the Mississippi
childhood without diabetes.
reliving a disrespectful youth
where a Black girl could be messy
and nothing else.

on the fifth day cancer came
like a double text from the IRS.
seizing assets you never owned to
begin with; a bad bitch with one titty
is just altar-less church empty

when all you're left with is disease
you drink a Pepsi three times a day.
powder the pills into your food.
carry your heaven to the psych ward
and don't apologize
if you bump a bitch on the way in.

she boils a pot of Fabuloso on the stove,
and presses the needle into
the Luther Vandross vinyl.
paints the whole place orange
and waits for the voices to come
crawling out of her mind,
whispering, ready to play.

Assata

for Page May

people hear Assata's Daughters
& expect us Black academy pretty
Rosa Parks proper
they don't understand

the Black woman's burden is silence,
not a study or science,
but a privatized poison
a Black code to throw blows with

we want an out
we've had it with Chicago white folk
their deer-in-headlight hatred
cringing bodies and clutched purse

my girls can't afford to sit
can't afford a peaceful protest
against the cop academy/prison industrial
we have a court date with the complex

our friends free labor behind fences
our families flip bricks and end up in boxes
our baby daddies spoon feed
then spill into gang war

we only know pop out for our people
we only know wig-snatch whiteness
by any means necessary
for Assata's, without question.

Scott, in the Seat Behind Me, Compliments My Hair After Taking Pictures and Complaining About Its Capacity

Aspen, Colorado

nope, I don't wash it often.
yes, it's here on a scholarship, and yes,
        I know it's big.
my hair so big it needed an extra seat
on the flight over.
my hair so big, she got a donk
you can look, but don't touch,
my hair gets a pat down
at the airport, they still can't tell
my whole body is the bomb.

you know, scott, it's sweet of you
to want the good graces of my hair,
after we've already seen you snap the photo,
body shame my hair in a text to your cousins.
you Bo Derek subtweet through a blonde cornrow
you want my hair hoodrich glam, pitbull tame,
star on the sidewalk of a newspaper clip
it's autograph in the burn book
of Tennessee's lawmakers.

oh scott, we know men like you
the power it must make you feel
to tabloid the child star of my scalp,
a lost soul screaming in a sea of white
noise. something worth noting,

21

should you be twice lucky
enough to meet hair so big,
bring a photo release form.
hair like mine don't fuck with paparazzi.

FUBU

After Danez Smith

everybody here
knows summer
is just an excuse
for Vaseline.
its desire for ash,
or forced opening.
the sun's sweet whisper
against the elbow:
shine, nigga.
the bullet's sweet whisper
against skin
forced open

we are frightened
of nothing.
the neighborhood
unfuckwittable
spits laughter
that splits rocks.

back home, mothers
cradle us on t-shirts.
our cribs a street memorial.
our names hot combs
ripping through air:
spread, nigga.
squad singing
across forgotten
earth, reclaiming
all the territory
renamed white space.

yes, some of us
used to gang bang
and still do.
some of us went
to college to trap,
expand our clientele
to folk who don't
know a frisking hand
on the walk home.
some of us got good
jobs in firms
or agencies.

still, we all ended
up here
and human—
sucking our fingers
free from hot Cheeto
crumbs
bumping entire albums
of slurping
and smacking lips—

even if back home
we are just another
buried body
even if back home
our names are all
that remain.

I Am Windy City

After Jayne Cortez's "I am New York City"

i am windy city. here is my tomato-head-baton-scattered badge and
    blue. i got my cousin's ears
of corn gentrifrying in the melting pot. my mouth a mercury lake i
    baptized Jean Baptiste
in a barn fire. I am windy city of red meat. stocked yards of men in
    factories inside my belly
a jungle of segregated joints. rub my Navy Pores with the blood of
    betadine boys making
steel and stealing it. i am windy city of cabrini green giants. hear my
    newport throat croak

an eight-hour work day. a haymarket rally in the projects. pipe
bomb at pullman's pied piper. i work for no one. i am windy city of
bloody gums. my teeth a collection of patina-coated churches. my
ferris wheel earrings too chicana for the rest of white-ass illinois.
my boys cleansed the white city with a storm of gunpowder tears. i
am windy city only dressed in white on valentines for all my lovers
were massacred at the hands of chiraq. a man i don't know who
keeps trying to wife me. chiraq is boo boo da fool and the foolish
who bool with peeping toms who have license to stripsearch. chiraq
turn churches into resale gun stores. chiraq a trap song siren-ade
sung into the wrong ear. chiraq city of lost boys under the hood.
chiraq could never take my face value of royal flush into the chicago
river. my leaning sears tower of deep dish pizza. my Heineken and
soulfood. gout feet tap dancing barefoot with my hotheaded friends.
my confetti fleshed comrades. come break bread with me.

What to Do When the Wells Is Turned into a Facebook Group

go to church and pray, thank The Lord
for finally getting rid of the police
cameras. log into your childhood home
and be grateful for thick walls.
now you can argue in the privacy of a
direct message. now you can post
on the block and not watch your back.
now shorty who said it was poppin'
next time she see you gotta send a friend
request. ain't this the life? a playdate
in the comfort of your bedroom.
no more waiting on the front porch
of purgatory. daddy always shows up
when you type his name. a vigil
is just comments under a digitized obituary.
we are still dying but in better places.
shit, if I knew this was the price I had to pay
for permanence, I would've stopped going
outside a long time ago. who needs liberation
when your prison is comfortable?

On Foe Nem Grave

the first time you said it,
all the boys looking for a place
to rest found one.

tongue or twilight zone,
six feet under a sucking tooth,
an empty lot altar
of tithes to pay onna guys.
all the ground Chicago
is missing onna mans.

your gums a burial site for the niggas
Uncle Chris told you to stay away from.
niggas like him, niggas that stay banging—
body a gamble even in the afterlife.

Chicago a casino
where everyone plays a chip with a name
on a table of bids and broken promises,
an offering to merch and commerce.

the second we forget the matter
in a Black life it becomes gas.

"I only wanna make you happy   on foe nem grave."
"An asswhooping next time I see you   on foe nem grave."
"I promise I don't mess with shorty   on foe nem grave."
"I would die for my niggas   on foe nem grave."

you say the words and do the work of forgetting
the heads you place your bets on.

say the words and work the pain away.
work a price tag on your lips.
your debt in the mouth of a shorty
just trying to survive the space you left.

Funeral Scene Where It Isn't Raining (a retelling)

after Eve Ewing

Graphite died on a hot September night. Her spirit rose from her body like a bird fleeing a falling tree, traversing the green and yellow bathroom walls. She flew over the empty plain we used to call home, moonwalked across the McCormick place bridge, and into the Uber on 22nd street, where her granddaughter received the news. Her granddaughter hung up the phone and fell into the arms of the car door, weeping into a cup holder. The sun fell with her granddaughter's breath, the driver redirected the route. The car rises off the ground, the driver pulls the gear shift one notch past L. The car tilts upward, engine smoking like the head of a cigarette. The car spins the granddaughter's brain back in time. Gyrating as though driving through a giggle. It is 1998 and Graphite died years before of old age. The granddaughter exits the vehicle and the doctor shouts, "It's a girl!" It is a selfish new world. The granddaughter cries as Jay-Z raps "Hard Knock Life," but the granddaughter will never know.

Post-Demolition Manifesto

what rose from the ashes was a hoe
/horn of plenty, a body for nobody(s).
for windows and loud tenants.
for juke jam on the front porch of this flat ass.
for a nigga who appreciates the effort.
may I be the landlord. queen of my own eviction.
may the safe passage of my back be for my poly and polluted
women, condoms in the lawn of their likeness,
section 8 responsibly. call me a twin tower with no repairman,
a building of butch girls trappin' out the bando.

we spit game for survival, petition for
rent extension running down our
fire escape mouths. always filled and fleeing,
fighting back the urge. to say something
is to make yourself quiet in the ear of a bulldozer:
the city that tries to tax my stairways.
the city that forecloses on a kiss.
the city that says you have to choose between your body
and the people that love it.

my grandmother has already blessed me with my own hell.
a christening for coming out. and open
is how I choose to leave my front door. is how my partner loves me.
true to self even in plural. when my grandmother died I became
graphite,
because nobody ever tried to gentrify a pencil, because she was. I am
the wreckage rented out,
for no crew to try to reclaim/rebuild
for me.

My Gay-Ass Poem

Graphite couldn't make it to the writing of this poem. I am not angry
with her.
the words *that's against God Pat Pat* roll backwards up her throat &
her mouth becomes a borderless country. God is made in my image
and so must be a dyke who don't fuck with the religion of geography.

I am the sun and the moon scissor fucking
in God's master bathroom. I derby skate in a ring of fire
while niggas on earth try to reduce me to a rainbow.
everyday another part of me
becomes a cautionary tale turned law.

I learned my body was dangerous the day after my first period.
a nigga thought he saw woman and tried to shatter it with a whistle,
see if cunts could crack at high frequency. everyday, another nigga
took turns trying to run me a margin. still ain't figured out a border
ain't shit but a word used to cut corners, and my body has none.

I am the reason all the bad words exist. does that mean I should stay
silent so my family will be at peace? my pussy won't allow it,
she is a vigilante hands around the neck of a perimeter. if my words
leave you hungry to chew me out, my areolas are a free meal program
come and eat to the core of this rotten girl. when the revolution
comes,
I won't be sorry for my body, the color of dirty things, young, Black,
weird and gay. I know Graphite loved me, regardless.

I Do This For

My mama, Mama Tiahanna, for birthing and bathing me, for letting me talk my bullshit, for never wanting me to stay in a child's place, I love you.

My sisters, Anaya and Leilani, Dekuria, Danavia, Chloe, & Haley. Keep the story pushing, never lose your will to be whoever the world says you can't.

Kamari, for motivation, for love, for muse, for firsts, including always being my first and most trusted reader.

Ms. Barfield's fourth grade class, for letting me know that I should do anything with my words besides sing them.

Auntie Shanicka, Auntie Ray-Ray, Auntie Jelly, Uncle Chris.
My grandparents who never actually regarded the "grand-" part of the word &
the rest of my family and friends who stay gassin' me.

The late Mama Brenda, who taught me multiplicity.
My tirelessly giving mentors & teachers Mama Berg, Jamila, Fati, Bee Kapri, RJ, José, Jasmine, Heather, Nate, Kevin, Avery, Emily, Lufrano, Hazzard, and many more.

Everybody who published these baby poems: *South Side Weekly, Breaking the Chains,* & *Chicago Tribune.*

Haymarket Press, because literacy is one of the most radical forms of activism.

Assata's Daughters, because they do this for me, and Sandra, Nita,

Nisa, Dream, Anna, Simone, Selah, Nayana, Asha, and all the Chicago Black Girls without a thing but steam.

Young Chicago Authors, where I was given an engine. Anna, Mariah, Tammy, Kesha, keep doing the work.
Urban Word, thank you for giving me the opportunity to serve as the Nation's Youth Poet Laureate.

Gwendolyn Brooks College Prep's Poetry Slam Team, Arielle, Destiny, Moriah, Gabby, Seanba, James, Jerome, Anaya, Dajona, Kennedy, Elijah, Allie Gillick.

Louder Than a ~~Bomb~~ BOOB Squad, KZ, AJ, Keyante, Jalen, Antwon, E'mon, Sara, Sammy, Suubi, Melinda, Kee, Banu, Kara, Marcus, Luis, Vicky, Levi, Stephanie, Deja, Kenny, Jahnari, and Stephanie.

The literary icons that keep me alive & audacious, Octavia Butler, Safia Elhillo, Zora Neale Hurston, Rita Dove, Gwendolyn Brooks, Patricia Smith, Assata Shakur, Lucille Clifton, Tracy K. Smith, Mahogany Browne, Amanda Gorman, Ray Bradbury, Toni Morrison, Dana Davidson, Claudia Rankine, Danez Smith, Saba, Noname, Martin Espada, Fatimah Asghar, Jamila Woods, Eve Ewing, Jose Olivarez, Nate Marshall, Britteney "Black Rose" Kapri, Kush Thompson, Kevin Coval, Kara Jackson, & many many more.

Rukmini, Mila, & William.

everyone who edited until my poems were a little less shitty.
everyone who read these semi shitty poems.

If not for God, I wouldn't have any of these wonderful people to thank.

Chicago.

ABOUT THE AUTHOR

Filmmaker, activist, and Chicago and National Youth Poet Laureate, Patricia Frazier uses art to express issues of urgency and celebrate young and Black political movements. Her work appears in *Chicago Magazine, South Side Weekly, New City Lit 50, Vogue,* and has been performed with Apple Inc. at the Library of Congress, Federal Hall and more. She is an organizer with Assata's Daughters, an intergenerational, grassroots organization of women and femme-identifying folks working to deepen, sustain, and escalate the Black Lives Matter movement. A Davis-Putter scholar, she currently studies cinema arts and sciences at Columbia College Chicago.

ABOUT HAYMARKET BOOKS

Haymarket Books is a radical, independent, nonprofit book publisher based in Chicago.

Our mission is to publish books that contribute to struggles for social and economic justice. We strive to make our books a vibrant and organic part of social movements and the education and development of a critical, engaged, international left.

We take inspiration and courage from our namesakes, the Haymarket martyrs, who gave their lives fighting for a better world. Their 1886 struggle for the eight-hour day—which gave us May Day, the international workers' holiday—reminds workers around the world that ordinary people can organize and struggle for their own liberation. These struggles continue today across the globe—struggles against oppression, exploitation, poverty, and war.

Since our founding in 2001, Haymarket Books has published more than five hundred titles. Radically independent, we seek to drive a wedge into the risk-averse world of corporate book publishing. Our authors include Noam Chomsky, Arundhati Roy, Rebecca Solnit, Angela Y. Davis, Howard Zinn, Amy Goodman, Wallace Shawn, Mike Davis, Winona LaDuke, Ilan Pappé, Richard Wolff, Dave Zirin, Keeanga-Yamahtta Taylor, Nick Turse, Dahr Jamail, David Barsamian, Elizabeth Laird, Amira Hass, Mark Steel, Avi Lewis, Naomi Klein, and Neil Davidson. We are also the trade publishers of the acclaimed Historical Materialism Book Series and of Dispatch Books.

CPSIA information can be obtained
at www.ICGtesting.com
Printed in the USA
JSHW042057080221
11722JS00006B/121